# What Is It?

Written by Dorothy Avery

Red

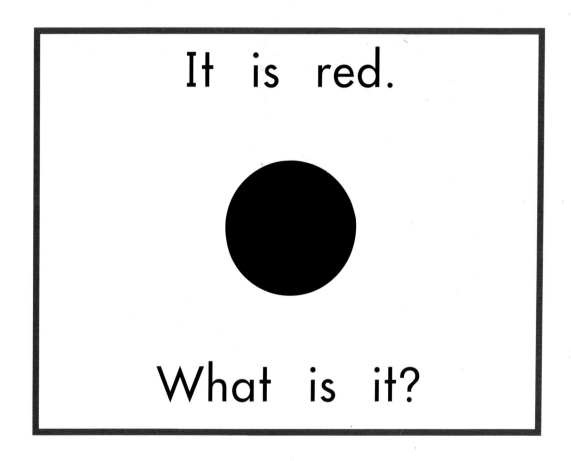

It is red.

What is it?

It is a strawberry.

Green

It is green.

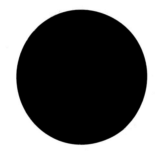

What is it?

It is an avocado.

Yellow

# It is yellow.

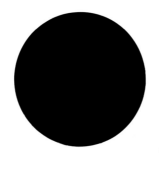

# What is it?

It is a banana.

It is red and sweet. What is it?

It is green and sour. What is it?

It is yellow and hot. What is it?

It is a strawberry.
It is a lime.
It is a chili pepper.